GETTING TO KNOW THE WORLD'S GREATEST ARTISTS

MARC
CHAGALL

WRITTEN AND ILLUSTRATED BY MIKE VENEZIA

CHILDREN'S PRESS®
A DIVISION OF GROLIER PUBLISHING
NEW YORK   LONDON   HONG KONG   SYDNEY
DANBURY, CONNECTICUT

To Mike and Liz, keep your heads gently floating.

Cover: *I and the Village,* by Marc Chagall. 1911. Oil on canvas. 192.1 x 151.4 cm.
Mrs. Simon Guggenheim Fund/Photograph 2000. © Museum of Modern Art, New York.

Colorist for illustrations: Kathy Hickey

Library of Congress Cataloging-in-Publication Data

Venezia, Mike.
    Marc Chagall / written and illustrated by Mike Venezia.
      p.   cm. — (Getting to know the world's greatest artists)
    Summary: Discusses the life and work of the artist Chagall, from
his birth in Russia to his death at the age of ninety-seven.
    ISBN 0-516-21055-6 (lib. bdg.) 0-516-27041-9 (pbk.)
    1. Chagall, Marc. 1887-1985. Juvenile literature. 2. Artists—Russia
(Federation) Biography Juvenile literature.   [1. Chagall, Marc.
1887-1985. 2. Artists.] I. Title. II. Series: Venezia, Mike.
Getting to know the world's greatest artists.
N6999.C46V46   2000
709'.2—dc21
[B]   99-41807
                                                    CIP
                                                    AC

Self-Portrait with Seven Fingers, by Marc Chagall. 1911. On loan from Netherlands Institute for Cultural Heritage. © Stedelijk Museum, Amsterdam.

Marc Chagall was born in the Russian city of Vitebsk in 1887. He used memories of his childhood and images from his dreams to come up with a magical, beautiful, and sometimes very mysterious kind of art.

Over Vitebsk, by Marc Chagall. 1914. Oil on paper mounted on canvas. 70.8 x 90.2 cm.
Gift of Sam and Ayala Zacks, 1970/Estate of Chagall/Photograph by Carlo Catenazzi, AGO.
© Art Gallery of Ontario, Toronto/Musée des beaux-arts de l'Ontario.

Marc Chagall and his family lived in the Jewish section of Vitebsk, which was more like a small village than a city. To Marc, Vitebsk seemed like a stage in a theater. He thought of the people there as actors acting out a mysterious, wonderful play.

I and the Village, by Marc Chagall. 1911. Oil on canvas. 192.1 x 151.4 cm. Mrs. Simon Guggenheim Fund/
Photograph 2000. © Museum of Modern Art, New York.

People who lived in Vitebsk were very poor and had hard lives. The happiest times were during celebrations, like weddings and religious holidays. In many of Marc's paintings, people who are happy are shown floating in the air, free from their problems.

The Walk, by Marc Chagall. Russian State Museum, St. Petersburg, Russia © ARS, NY. Photograph © Art Resource, NY/Scala.

Marc often painted animals doing things that people do. This seemed normal to Marc because he grew up listening to lots of Russian folk stories and fairy tales in which animals were humanlike.

Green Violinist (Violiniste), by Marc Chagall. 1923-24. Oil on canvas. 198 x 108.6 cm. Gift of Solomon R. Guggenheim, 1937/The Solomon R. Guggenheim Foundation, NY/Photograph by David Heald. © Solomon R. Guggenheim Museum, New York.

Marc Chagall had seven sisters and one brother. His father was a fish seller and his mother owned a small grocery store.

There were always lots of fun aunts and uncles around. One of Marc's favorites was his Uncle Neuch. Uncle Neuch played the violin. Marc said that when Uncle Neuch danced around the room playing, Marc became so happy that his head would gently float off his body and follow his uncle around. Marc Chagall was a great dreamer.

Marc always loved animals. He enjoyed talking to the goats, chickens, and friendly cows that roamed around his village.

Marc talked to the stars in the sky, too. He thought of them as his friends.

Marc noticed that the stars always waited for him wherever he went. He said he sometimes apologized for keeping them waiting for such a long time way up there in the sky.

The Sabbath, by Marc Chagall. 1910. Oil on canvas. 90 x 95 cm. Rheinisches Bildarchiv Köln.
© Museum Ludwig Köln, Cologne, Germany.

Marc Chagall never saw a painting
or drawing until he was thirteen years
old. Art and artists weren't a part of most
people's lives in his small village.

One day in school, Marc saw a boy copy a picture out of a book. Marc couldn't believe his eyes! He didn't know a person could do such a thing. Right away Marc tried copying pictures himself. He loved drawing, and put his artwork up all over the house.

It was during this time that Marc Chagall decided he would be an artist. At first his parents thought it was a crazy idea. They hardly knew what an artist was. But Marc was so excited that he finally convinced his mother to let him take art lessons. Marc found an art school in the busier part of Vitebsk.

The Wedding, by Marc Chagall. 1909. Private Collection, Switzerland/Photograph by Erich Lessing.
© Art Resource, NY.

Marc learned to draw mostly by copying plaster statues. In 1907, when he was twenty years old, Marc went to St. Petersburg, the capital city of Russia. There, he was able to study with better teachers and see the work of well-known Russian artists. He began to paint his first mysterious works from his memory.

La Rue Montorgueil, Festival of June 30, 1878,
by Claude Monet. Musée d'Orsay, Paris, France
© Art Resource, NY/Giraudon.

While in St. Petersburg, Marc also learned about Paris, France. Paris was a city where many of the world's best artists went to study.

Marc Chagall decided to move to Paris in 1911. He loved the people, beautiful buildings, and restaurants he found there. The most important thing Marc found in Paris though, was the light.

Roofs at Collioure, by Henri Matisse. 1905. Hermitage
Museum, St. Petersburg, Russia. © ARS, NY.
Photograph © Art Resource, NY.

Everything seemed to glitter and sparkle with light in Paris! Marc understood how French artists like Claude Monet and Henri Matisse were able to fill their paintings with light and color. Soon Marc Chagall started adding more color to his paintings. He found it gave them more life, and they seemed to glow from the inside!

The Cattle Dealer, by Marc Chagall. 1912. Kunstmuseum, Basel, Switzerland © Art Resource, NY/Scala.

When Marc Chagall was starting out in Paris, he and his artist friends were very poor. Because they couldn't afford canvases, they sometimes had to paint on tablecloths, bed sheets, or even the back of their pajamas. In *The Violinist,* you can even see the pattern of the tablecloth Marc used!

The Violinist, by Marc Chagall. 1912-13. On loan from the Netherlands Institute for Cultural Heritage. © Stedelijk Museum, Amsterdam.

Fiddlers were very important to Marc Chagall. They reminded him of his Uncle Neuch and happy times from his childhood. Also, Marc thought of fiddlers as mystical leaders in Russian Jewish villages.

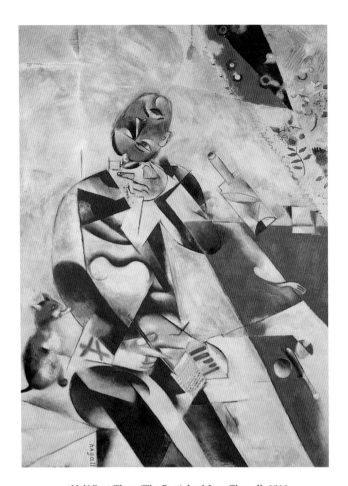

Marc was painting some of his most exciting works now. Sometimes he was influenced by other artists' works, such as Pablo Picasso's cubist paintings. Marc kept his work original, though, by sticking with his idea of using dreams and memories from his past.

The Soldier Drinks (Le Soldat Boit), by Marc Chagall. 1911-12. Oil on canvas. 109.1 x 94.5 cm. The Solomon R. Guggenheim Foundation, NY/Photograph by David Heald. © Solomon R. Guggenheim Museum.

This may have been Marc Chagall's most important decision as an artist.

The Bolshevik, by Boris Kustodiev. 1920. Tretyakov Gallery, Moscow, Russia © Art Resource, NY/Scala.

After spending four years in Paris, Marc decided to go home for a short visit. Just after he arrived in Vitebsk, World War I began, and right after that, the Russian Revolution began. Marc wasn't allowed to leave Russia during this time, and his short visit lasted seven years!

These were important years for Marc Chagall, though. Marc learned what Russian Revolutionary artists were doing.

Music, by Marc Chagall. 1920. Tretyakov Museum, Moscow, Russia/Photograph by Itar-Tass. © Sovfoto/Eastfoto.

Dance, by Marc Chagall. 1920. Tretyakov Museum, Moscow, Russia, © Sovfoto/Eastfoto.

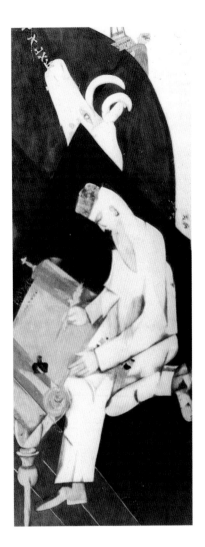

Literature, by Marc Chagall. 1920. Tretyakov Museum, Moscow, Russia, © Sovfoto/Eastfoto.

He made paintings for the new Russian government and headed up an art program, organizing museums and putting on art shows. Marc also painted a huge mural for the Jewish theater in the city of Moscow.

Theatre, by Marc Chagall. 1920. Tretyakov Museum, Moscow, Russia, © Sovfoto/Eastfoto.

The Birthday (l'Anniversaire), by Marc Chagall. 1915. Oil on cardboard. 80.6 x 99.7 cm.
Acquired through the Lillie P. Bliss Bequest. Photograph 2000.
© Museum of Modern Art, New York.

Maybe the most important thing to happen to Marc Chagall during his long stay in Russia was falling in love and marrying his sweetheart, Bella Rosenfeld. Marc and Bella were crazy about each other.

Even during years of war, Marc had some of his happiest times. He showed his joy of life and love for Bella in many of his paintings.

Double Portrait with Wineglass, by Marc Chagall. 1917-18. Oil on canvas. Musée National d'Art Moderne, Centre National d'Art et de Culture George Pompidou, Paris, France/Photograph by Erich Lessing. © Art Resource, NY.

Peasant Life, by
Marc Chagall. 1925.
Oil on canvas.
39 3/8 x 31 1/2 in.
Room of Contemporary
Art Fund, 1941.
© Albright-Knox Art
Gallery, Buffalo, NY.

In 1922, Marc Chagall was finally able
to leave Russia. He moved back to Paris
with Bella and their daughter, Ida.
Marc became busier than ever—painting,
illustrating books, and exhibiting his
work. He and his family lived in France
until World War II began.

Things weren't safe for them now. Adolf Hitler, the German dictator who started the war, was planning to take over France. Hitler didn't like modern art or artists at all. He made sure their works were taken out of museums, and he sometimes even had paintings destroyed!

But worse than that, Adolf Hitler hated anyone of the Jewish faith.

White Crucifixion, by Marc Chagall. 1938. Oil on canvas. 154.3 x 139.7 cm.
Gift of Alfred S. Alschuler, 1946.925. © Art Institute of Chicago.

Obsession, by Marc Chagall. 1943. Photograph by Philippe Migeat. © Musée National d'Art Moderne, Centre National d'Art et de Culture Georges Pompidou.

Luckily, Marc Chagall was invited to stay in the United States at that time. The Chagalls left France right away.

In America, Marc's paintings changed. His works started to show how upset he was about the war.

Autour d'elle, by Marc Chagall. 1945. Oil on canvas. 1.31 x 1.09 m. Musée National d'Art Moderne, Centre National d'Art et de Culture Georges Pompidou, Paris, France. © ARS, NY. Photograph © Art Resource, NY/Giraudon.

Just before World War II ended, a terrible thing happened. Bella became ill and died. This was the worst time of Marc Chagall's life. He didn't paint for months. When he finally began painting again, he used his powerful, mysterious colors and images to show his sadness.

As time went on, Marc Chagall got back to using happier colors and images in many of his paintings. He began creating prints, stage designs, and ceramics, too.

Marc Chagall also made wonderful stained-glass windows. His swirling colors, lit from behind by sunlight, are amazing to see. They seem to fill the area with color and make you feel like you're part of his magical world.

The Juggler, by Marc Chagall. 1943. Oil on canvas. 109.9 x 79.1 cm. Gift of Mrs. Gilbert W. Chapman, 1952.1005. © The Art Institute of Chicago.

Marc Chagall lived to be ninety-seven years old. He had an amazing imagination, mixing scenes from his dreams with those of the real world. Throughout Marc Chagall's life, his art showed the images he remembered from the time he was a small boy.

Works of art in this book can be seen at the following places:

Albright-Knox Gallery, Buffalo, New York
Art Gallery of Toronto, Ontario, Canada
Art Institute of Chicago, Chicago, Illinois
Carmen Bores Gallery, Madrid, Spain
Hermitage Museum, St. Petersburg, Russia
Kunstmuseum, Basel, Switzerland
Kunstsammlung Nordrhein-Westfalen, Düsseldorf, Germany
Musée National d'Art Moderne, Centre National d'Art et de Culture Georges Pompidou, Paris, France
Musée d'Orsay, Paris, France

Museum Ludwig Köln, Cologne, Germany
Museum of Modern Art, New York, New York
Parliament, Jersualem, Israel
Philadelphia Museum of Art, Philadelphia
Pushkin Museum of Fine Arts, Moscow, Russia
Russian State Museum, St. Petersburg, Russia
Solomon R. Guggenheim Museum, New York, New York
Stedelijk Museum, Amsterdam, The Netherlands
Tate Gallery, London, Great Britain
Tretyakov Gallery, Moscow, Russia